OUR • WORLD • MY • ROOTS
NIGERIA

WRITTEN BY ANNA MAKANDA & SHARMANE BARRETT
ILLUSTRATED BY NATÀLIA JUAN ABELLÓ

OUR DEDICATIONS

In Anna's words:

To my parents, for always believing in me and encouraging me to shoot for the moon. To my mum, for teaching me that in order to know who you are, you must know where you come from. To my husband, for being my absolute rock through thick and thin. To my two beautiful children, who inspire me every day.

In Sharmane's words:

To my parents and my sisters for being my biggest challengers, as well as supporters in life. To my nine amazing nieces and nephews, for being my constant reminder that I need to be a better me for all of the little eyes that are watching.

To all the little explorers,
may you always remember to:

BE CURIOUS

BE CONFIDENT

BE KIND

BE YOU

CONTENTS

FACTFILE — 01

MAP OF NIGERIA — 03

INTRO — 05

HELLO — 07

WELCOME — 09

MEET MY FAMILY — 11

WHERE WE LIVE — 15

LET'S EXPLORE — 17

LET'S GO TO SCHOOL — 33

LET'S PLAY	37
LET'S LEARN	39
LET'S SAY	43
LET'S EAT	45
LET'S CELEBRATE	47
LET'S GET LUCKY	57
LET'S DREAM	59
GOODBYE	63
FLAG	65
HISTORY	66

NORTH AMERICA

EUROPE

AFRICA

SOUTH AMERICA

NIGERIA

ANTARCTICA

LOCATION
Nigeria is a country in West Africa. It is bordered by Niger to the north, Chad in the northeast, Cameroon in the east and Benin in the west. Its southern coast faces the Gulf of Guinea, which is a part of the Atlantic Ocean.

Size: 923,769 km²
Capital: Abuja
Currency: Naira (NGN)
Population: 206 million (2020)
Major Cities: Lagos, Abuja, Kano, Warri, Port Harcourt
Highest Point: Chappal Waddi Mountain at 2,419 m

WEATHER
Nigeria has a tropical climate with variable rainy and dry seasons where the temperature ranges between 12 and 38°C, depending on the region and the season. There are two seasons inland:

Northern Nigeria
Rainy Season: June-September
Dry season: October-May

Southern Nigeria
Rainy Season: February and April-October
Dry season: March and November-January

The dry season is accompanied by a lot of dust from the Sahara Desert (otherwise known as Harmattan).

LANGUAGES
English is the official language in Nigeria, but there are hundreds of languages spoken. Three of the most widely spoken languages are Yoruba, Igbo, and Hausa.

RELIGION
Approximately 50% of the population in Nigeria are Muslim, 40% are Christian, and the remaining 10% follow tribal beliefs.

KANO

NIGER

KAMUKU NATIONAL PARK

JOS PLATEAU

ADO AWAYE LAKE

FARIN RUWA FALLS

ABUJA

BENUE

ANCIENT IFE CITY

LAGOS

WARRI

PORT HARCOURT

LAKE CHAD

SUKUR CULTURAL LANDSCAPE

KUMARI

CHAPPAL WADDI

KEEP AN EYE OUT FOR

- Capital: Abuja
- Major Cities: Lagos, Kano, Warri, and Port Harcourt
- Mountains: Chappal Waddi, Tsaunin Kwaiki, and Kumari
- Rivers: Niger River and Benue River
- Lake Chad
- Jos Plateau
- Farin Ruwa Waterfall
- Ancient Ife City
- Sukur Cultural Landscape
- Ado Awaye Lake

ARE YOU EXCITED ABOUT GOING ON AN ADVENTURE?

Join us on a journey across land and sea, taking you to Nigeria: the land of hidden treasures, often referred to as the 'Giant of Africa'. It is a country filled with sensational scenery and wondrous wildlife. This book will guide you through the country's geography, people, culture, and beyond.

But there's more there than meets the eye: Nigeria has a huge diversity of languages, communities, beliefs, and traditions. The people of Nigeria are known for being very confident and vibrant and they have a strong sense of pride in their nationality.

You may be surprised to find that even though
Nigeria is filled with lots of things that are different
to where you live, there are many similarities too.

Nigeria is almost four times the size of England
and home to over 200 million people who speak
hundreds of different languages.

Perhaps you have Nigerian heritage and you want to
learn more about your roots, or simply want to learn
more about this amazing country. You will find some
of the many special things about Nigeria in this book,
but there is so much more to discover. We hope that
you will be able to travel all the way to Nigeria
and beyond someday.

THE OFFICIAL LANGUAGE OF NIGERIA IS ENGLISH.

This is how to say 'Hello' in three of the other widely spoken languages:

Some of the other languages are: Fulfulde, Gbagyi, Ijaw, Mesiere Anaang, Tiv, and Kanuri.

Throughout the pages of this book you will find many words and phrases translated in:

Igbo (red)
Yoruba (blue)
Hausa (green)

Ẹ PẸ̀LẸ́ O
(YORUBA)

SANNU
(HAUSA)

MEET MY FAMILY

When I am home from boarding school, I live with my three brothers, Adedayo (Ade), Oladele, and Temidayo; my sister, Aina; my parents; and my grandparents. We live in Lagos. We speak Yoruba and English. I have many aunts, uncles, and cousins too who live in different areas in Nigeria. Let me introduce you to my...

Family
Ìdílé   Ezinulo   Iyali

Mum
Iya   Nne   Uwa

Dad
Bàbá   Nna   Uba

Grandad
Bàbá Bàbá   Nna nna   Kaka

Grandma
Ìyá Ìyá   Nne nne   Kaka

Uncle
Arákùnrin Bàbá
Nwanne nne nwoke   Kawu

Auntie
Arábìnrin Bàbá
Nwanne nne nwaanyị
Goggo

Sister
Arábìnrin
Nwanne Nwaanyi
Yar uwa

Cousin
Ìyá Ẹni Lóbìnrin
Nwa nwanne nne
Ɗan uwa

Brother
Arákùnrin
Nwanne nwoke
Ɗan uwa

Friend
Ọ̀rẹ́   Enyi   Kawa

NKECHI'S FAMILY ALSO LIVE IN LAGOS;

they speak Igbo and English.

My parents and Nkechi's parents are good friends as our dads do business together. We call Nkechi's mum 'da' or 'dada' (big aunty or big sister) and her dad 'de / dede' (big uncle / big brother). Baba says that this is the way we show our respect to those who are older than us.

HALIMA'S FAMILY LIVE IN KADUNA;

they speak Hausa and English.

Nkechi and I became friends with Halima at school. We all board at the same international school because our parents travel a lot for work. We don't often see Halima outside school because Kaduna is so far from Lagos.

DID YOU KNOW?

Most Nigerian names have a meaning. This is what our traditional names mean:

Abiola – One born into wealth (in Yoruba)
Adedayo – The crown has turned to joy (in Yoruba)
Nkechi – God's own (in Igbo)
Halima – Gentle heart (in Hausa)

WHERE WE LIVE

Ade and I live in a terraced house within a compound in Lagos.

...but we also have a large bungalow that Baba built in our parents' home village of Anambra.

Our cousins, Emmanuel and Blessing, live in a mansion in Abuja.

Many people used to live in traditional rural homes, made of bamboo, vines, and mud with palm roofs. These have been replaced by large groups of small wooden houses.

Our cousins Jide, Ife, and Neze live in a small wooden house in a village in Abuja.

Home
Ilé   Ulo   Gida

LET'S EXPLORE

LANDSCAPES

Ade and I love visiting different parts of Nigeria to see our family. Once we get out of the city, the views are beautiful. Sometimes Iya and Bàbá take us on a road trip so that we can visit somewhere new. It is such an adventure. Here are some of the things we have seen...

Explore
Wádíí
Ikiri ihe
Yin nazari

MOUNTAINS

There are 20 mountains spread around Nigeria. The three largest are Chappal Waddi, Tsaunin Kwaiki, and Kumari.

RIVERS

There are over 40 rivers in Nigeria but the 2 main ones are:

The Niger River, which is the longest river in West Africa. It starts in Guinea and flows through Mali, Niger, Benin, and into Nigeria.
Q: How many leopards could fit along the length of the Niger River?
A: 2.6 million leopards – it's 4,179 km long

The Benue River is a third of the length of the Niger River and it starts in Northern Cameroon.
Q: How many leopards could fit along the length of the Benue River?
A: 875 thousand leopards – it's 1,400 km long

The Benue River meets the Niger River at Lokoja and flows into the Atlantic Ocean.

LAKES 🔍

There are more than 50 lakes in Nigeria, some are big and some are small. Most of them are natural lakes, whilst a few of them are man-made reservoirs. The biggest is Lake Chad which is a natural lake, as well as one of the largest lakes in Africa. If you're lucky, you might see a rare sea cow in one of Nigeria's lakes, or a hippopotamus or two hanging out at their favourite watering hole.

DID YOU KNOW?

A sea cow (also called a West African manatee) can grow to 4 m long and weighs almost 600 kg. They all have large, plump bodies; downturned snouts; short, rounded, paddle-like flippers; and a horizontal tail that they use to propel themselves around. Although they are found in 21 countries, African manatees are incredibly shy and very hard to find.

SAVANNAS

These grasslands are flat, open spaces with trees and grass that turn golden during the hot dry season. Two hundred years ago, it was possible to see many animals there, but the numbers have reduced due to hunting and loss of grassland. You can still see leopards, hyenas, and jackals.

WATERFALLS

There are several waterfalls in Nigeria including Matsirga Falls, Owu Falls, Assop Falls, and Awhum Falls. The largest waterfall in Nigeria is Farin Ruwa Falls. Some have cool pools to swim in and others have long winding roads leading up to the top where you can see the beautiful views.

FORESTS

There are two types of forests in Nigeria: rainforests and mangrove forests. These forests are mainly found in the southeast of Nigeria, particularly in the Niger River Delta where it often rains a lot.

PLATEAUS Q

A plateau is an area of flat land with a steep slope on at least one side. Nigeria has four plateaus: Adamawa Highlands, Mambilla Plateau, Obudu Plateau, and Jos Plateau. Jos Plateau has massive uneven rocks and extinct volcanoes. It is also home to the indigobird, which is not found anywhere else in the world.

Tree
Igi
Osisi
Itace

PLANTS AND TREES

There are thousands of different types of trees and plants in Nigeria. These include the umbrella tree, the nganda coffee tree, and the ube tree, which has a dark-blue coloured fruit called an African pear.

Everyone wants to have palm trees on their compound. We have lots at our home in Anambra and Ìyá Ìyá always tells her friends about how many we have. She uses the sap in the bark of the tree to make palm wine to serve to our guests at parties. We are only allowed to drink a small glass at weddings.

FACTS

A palm tree can live for up to 5,000 years and can grow to up to 20 m high. There are over 2,500 types of palm trees in the world.

Coconuts and bananas come from different types of palm trees. Dates and berries also grow on palm trees and other palms produce palm fruit.

In Nigeria, the palm provides many products including brooms, mats, baskets, oil, wine, and wood.

DID YOU KNOW?

Palm trees are not just found in tropical climates. Certain types of palm trees can grow in the snow in places such as the USA and Canada.

THE YELLOW TRUMPET

The *costus spectabilis* is the national flower of Nigeria, also known as the yellow trumpet. It can grow over 3 m high. It can be found in the country's forested areas and it symbolises the beauty of the nation. The yellow trumpet flower can be used to make medicine.

ANIMALS
Àwọn Ẹranko Ụmụ anụmanụ Dabbobi

When I was back home from school for the summer last year, Bàbá and Iya took the family on a trip to Yankari game reserve. Ade and I were so excited because we saw elephants, buffalos, hartebeest, baboons, monkeys, and a lion. We were so lucky to see the lion as there is only one left there now. He had been hiding in the shade because it was so hot.

DID YOU KNOW?

There are only 200–300 Cross River gorillas left in the wild, making them the most endangered great ape in Africa.

HERE ARE SOME OF THE MANY OTHER ANIMALS AND INSECTS YOU MAY FIND IN NIGERIA – SEE IF YOU CAN SPOT THEM:

Giraffe, leopard, red-eared guenon, white-throated guenon, dama gazelle, Senegal bushbaby, aardvark, forest elephant, Preuss's monkey, flamingo, Nigeria-Cameroon chimpanzee, African pygmy goose, comb-crested jacana, black-winged stilt, Egyptian plover, waterbuck, Cross River gorilla.

FARIN RUWA WATERFALL 🔍

Last summer I visited Farin Ruwa in Nasarawa with Nkechi and her family. It is one of the greatest attractions in Nigeria. Farin Ruwa is a Hausa term meaning 'white water'. The falls are more than 150 m high and 50 m wide. As the water crashes down, it gradually turns white because of its force. From a distance, the falls look like white smoke on the mountains.

DID YOU KNOW?

There are 11 different types of waterfalls in Nigeria, including a punchbowl, chute, and horsetail. The Farin Ruwa is a fan waterfall.

Nkechi, Halima, and I would like to visit some historical landmarks. The places that we hope to visit one day are:

THE ANCIENT IFE CITY 🔍
Ife is an ancient Yoruba city that is believed to be the birthplace of humankind. It is famous today for its magnificent bronze and terracotta metal head sculptures.

SUKUR CULTURAL LANDSCAPE 🔍
Sukur is a heritage site in the hills of the Mandara Mountains. Its stone structures, trees, and land have been kept the same for over 500 years. You can still see the palace of the local chief and the stables where his horses were kept, as well as the old village huts.

ADO AWAYE LAKE (OYO STATE) 🔍
The blue-green Ado Awaye Lake, also known as the 'sleeping lion', sits within a crest of rocks at the top of a hill. There are only two lakes like this in the world. There are around 350 steps to climb to get to the top and lots of historical spots to see along the way. At the top of the hill is a magnificent view over West Iseyin.

LEGEND HAS IT...
...the lake was so powerful that whatever prayer was made with its water would give magical results.

LAGOS

Lagos is the biggest city in Nigeria, it is known as 'the city that never sleeps'. It is on the southern coast and it spreads onto nearby Victoria Island. People call the island the 'Heart of the Nigerian Body'. Iya says one day we can go and take a look at some of the mansions on Victoria Island.

We love going into the city centre to see the soaring skyscrapers and listen to the hustle and bustle of people rushing around.

We have to get up very early to make sure that we are not sitting in traffic for hours and hours. Iya says that everyone in Nigeria wants to live in Lagos because it is a city of business and opportunity.

SOME GREAT PLACES TO SEE IN LAGOS ARE:

LEKKI MARKET
Here you will find a rich mix of arts and crafts from Nigeria and West Africa. It is perfect for wandering around or buying gifts and getting clothing made. Ade and I love to visit the markets and shopping malls as Iya often likes to treat us to something new.

NATIONAL THEATRE
The National Theatre is a beautiful building which is famous for performing arts. It has many halls for live stage performances and it hosts film and cultural shows, as well as art exhibitions and musical performances. Sometimes Iya goes to conferences there as well.

TARKWA BAY BEACH
Tarkwa Bay is a man-made beach near Lagos harbour. You can only get there by boat or water taxi. Day trips are popular because there are nice views and raft rides. You can also go swimming and there are even DJs there who play different types of music.

Bàbá has promised to take us there this summer.

LET'S GO TO SCHOOL

Nkechi, Halima, and I go to the same primary school in Ibadan. We are in third grade and Ade will soon be starting first grade. All our lessons are taught in English.

Our school has many classrooms and there are lots of fields where we run around and play sports. It is a boarding school which means we sleep there during the week and we go home at the weekend and for the holidays. The dorms are big – there are six children in each room – and we sleep on bunk beds. Nkechi tells lots of jokes at bedtime and we try not to laugh too loudly so that we don't get into trouble.

Our cousin, Jide, lives in an Abuja village. His school is quite different to ours as it is much smaller with less classrooms, which he tells us can get very full as everyone tries to squeeze in. His lessons are also taught in English. He walks to and from school every day.

School
Ilé-ìwé
Ụlọ akwụkwọ
Makaranta

Homework
Àṣetiléwá
Ihe ọmụme ụlọ akwụkwọ ana eme n' ụlọ
Aikin gida

Lesson
Èkọ́
Ihe ọmụmụ
Darasi

Teacher (Female)
Olùkọ́
Onye nkuzi nke nwanyị
Mallama

Student (Female)
Akẹ́kọ̀ọ́
Nwata akwụkwọ nwoke
Ɗaliba

Teacher (Male)
Olùkọ́
Onye nkuzi nke nwoke
Mallam

Student (Male)
Akẹ́kọ̀ọ́
Nwata akwụkwọ nwanyị
Ɗaliba

WE HAVE THE MOST FUN IN OUR...

MUSIC LESSONS

We play these instruments:

UBO AKA
(THUMB PIANO)

AGIDGBO
(LARGE THUMB PIANO BOX)

IKON
(XYLOPHONE)

DID YOU KNOW?

Football is one of the country's most popular sports. Nigeria was the first African country to win a gold medal in football at the Olympics. Its men's national team, the Super Eagles, has won the Africa Cup of Nations three times.

PE LESSONS

At school, there are lots of different sports like football and athletics. Boxing is very popular in Nigeria but we are not allowed to box at school. When I am at home, Bàbá takes me to a boxing club and I imagine myself punching like Anthony Joshua.

Play
Eré
Igwu egwu
Yin wasa

LET'S PLAY

During break time, we sometimes go to the fields where Halima loves to practice her backflips. We like to try too but are always falling over. We have to be careful as our teachers get cross if our uniform is dirty.

If we are not in the field, you will find us in the playground, either playing football or one of our favourite games, such as:

Boju Boju (hide and seek). The seeker sings: "Boju-boju, oloro nbo, shey kin shi? (Close your eyes, close your eyes, a masquerade is coming, should I open my eyes?)" while the rest of us hide. Then the seeker opens their eyes and tries to find us. The first one to be found is the seeker in the next game.

LET'S LEARN

NUMBERS

I have been helping Adowa learn how to count to ten.
Do you want to learn with us?

1
ỌKAN
OTU
ƉAYA

2
MÉJÌ
ABỤỌ
BIYU

3
MẸTA
ATỌ
UKU

4
MẸRIN
ANỌ
HUƉU

Learn
Láti kẹ́kọ̀ọ́
Imụta
Yin koyo

5 MÁRÙN / ISE / BIYAR

6 MẸFÀ / ISII / SHIDA

7 MÉJE / ASAA / BAKWAI

8 MÉJỌ / ASATỌ / TAKWAS

9 MẸSÀN / ITOOLU / TARA

10 MẸWÀÁ / IRI / GOMA

THE ALPHABET

Learning the alphabet is also fun! How many can you say?

A
E
AA
EI

B
B
BII
BII

C
S
SII
SII

D
D
DII
DI

E
I
EE
II

F
EF
FII
EF

G
J
GII
JI

H
EISH
HII
HEC

I
AI
II
AI

J
JE
JEE
JE

K
KE
KEE
KE

L
EL
LEE
EL

M
EM
MEE
AM

N
EN
NII
IN

O
O
OO
OU

P
P
PEE
FA

Q
KIU
KIO
KIW

R
AR
RII
AR

S
ES
SII
ES

T
T
TEE
TI

U
YU
UU
YU

V
V
VII
BI

W
DOUBLE YU
WEE
WAA

X
EKS
EKSI
AKS

Y
WAI
YII
WAI

Z
ZED
ZE
ZED

LET'S SAY

Here are some of our everyday words and phrases.
Why not try and say them?

HOW ARE YOU?

Báwo ni?
Kedu?
Kuke?

HOW OLD ARE YOU?

Ọmọ ọdún mélo ni ọ́?
Afọ ole ka ị dị?
Shekaranku nawa?

MY NAME IS...

...ni orúkọ mi
Aha m bụ...
Sunana...

I AM ... YEARS OLD

Ọmọ ọdún ... ni mí
Adị m afọ ...
Ina da shekara ...

GOOD MORNING

Káàárọ̀
Ututu ọma
Barka da safiya

GOOD AFTERNOON

Káàsán
Ehihie ọma
Barka da yini

GOOD NIGHT

O Dààrọ̀
Ka chifoo
Sai Gobe

I LOVE YOU

Mo nífẹ̀ rẹ
Ahụrụ m gị n'anya
Ina son ku

THANK YOU

Mo dúpẹ́
Imeela
Na Gode

PLEASE

Jọ̀wọ́
Biko
Don Allah

LET'S EAT
FOOD & DRINK

DID YOU KNOW?

The main difference between Nigerian Jollof and Ghanaian Jollof is the type of rice used. Nigerians use long grain rice whilst Ghanaians use aromatic basmati rice, both of which, give a different flavour.

ABI
I like to have bread and tea for breakfast. My favourite dinner is pounded yam and egusi soup which Iya makes for me when I am home from school.

NKECHI
I like to eat boiled plantain with stew for breakfast. My favourite dinner is yam with fish pepper soup.

Eat
Láti jẹ
Iri
A ci

HALIMA

For breakfast I like to have either Hausa koko – a deliciously spicy porridge made from millet – or Coco Pops. For dinner, my favourite is tuwo shinkafa. It is made of rice that is soft and sticky.

There are so many delicious snacks that we all love:

Puff puffs are like doughnuts but not sweet.

Chin Chin are crunchy, fried droplets of dough.

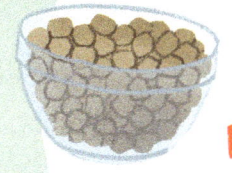

Shuku Shuku are little balls of coconut.

Kuli Kuli is a Hausa treat made from deep-fried, ground and spiced, roasted peanuts.

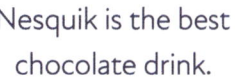

Guava, rose apple, tropical almonds, and pepper fruit are our tastiest fruits.

Nesquik is the best chocolate drink.

Zobo is a drink made from Hibiscus flowers.

LET'S CELEBRATE

We LOVE to celebrate! Yorubas are well-known for throwing big parties. We get together with family, friends, and neighbours. Sometimes Iya asks the tailor to come to our house so that we can get our outfits made for the party. When the day arrives, we get dressed up, eat tasty food, listen to music, and dance all day long. When we are not hosting our own parties, we can usually hear other people having one. My parents go to at least one party every weekend.

To Celebrate

Láti ṣe àjọyọ̀   Ime mmemme   A yi murna

Happy Birthday

Ẹ Kú Ọjọ́ Ìbí   Ezi ncheta ọmụmụ   Barka da Ranar Haihuwa

Party

Àpèjẹ náà   Mmemme ahụ   Bikin

Happy New Year

Obi ụtọ afọ ọhụrụ

CHRISTMAS

Christmas is the most exciting time of the year. It is always so much fun because we get new clothes, shoes, and jewellery. On Christmas morning, we go to church and in the afternoon, we drive back to our second house in our home village of Anambra, where Bàbá hosts a big party for the community.

Everyone stands and waves to welcome us back as we drive through the village. Sometimes it feels like we are famous. People come to eat, drink, dance, and listen to our stories of Lagos. We eat chicken and jollof rice for Christmas dinner. After dinner, we run around the compound, play tricks on people, and have fun with friends we haven't seen for a long time.

Halima's family are Muslim, so they don't celebrate Christmas. But when they celebrate a Muslim festival, there is always a big feast. Nkechi and I look forward to the delicious food Halima brings back to school after her weekend at home.

NATIONAL HOLIDAYS

We celebrate lots of national holidays in Nigeria. Bàbá Bàbá says that we have these days to honour important events and people in history. We have:

1st May – Labour Day – a day dedicated to workers around the world.

25th – 26th May – Eid ul Fitri – a day to celebrate the end of the Muslim fast, Ramadan.

12th June – Democracy Day – the date military rule ended in Nigeria in 1999. We celebrate the arrival of human rights and democracy in Nigeria.

30th July – Eid ul Kabir – is an Islamic festival to commemorate the willingness of the Prophet Ibrahim.

1st October – National Day – the day Nigeria gained independence.

29th October – Eid ul Maulud – a day to celebrate the Prophet Milad un Nabi's birthday.

We also celebrate birthdays, Easter, Christmas Day, Boxing Day, and New Year's Day.

On National Day, Bàbá Bàbá gathers us to watch the live broadcast of the President's speech on TV. We see the raising of the flag, the military parade, and the singing of the national anthem. There is always a big street party in our compound and everyone wears clothes in Nigeria's colours: green and white. Every year at school before National Day, we have a cultural show where we perform for our parents.

DID YOU KNOW?

Nigeria is one of the few countries around the world where there is a festival going on somewhere in the country, every single day of the year.

GIVING GIFTS

It is common for people to give gifts of food, fruit, nuts, or chocolate when invited to dinner, or to bring a gift for the children. People also like to gift traditional clothes.

DRESSING UP

Most of the time we wear the same kind of clothes that our cousins wear in the USA. On special occasions, the whole family wear traditional dress, especially when we go to a wedding. Men's hats are often a way to symbolise different tribes. It's fun to wear a kaba and asetam with a matching gele. The patterns and bright colours are very beautiful and striking. Usually, we wear outfits made of matching Ankara fabric. Ade loves to show off his Buba and Sokoto.

EATING

We eat chicken and jollof rice on special occasions but there is always an array of foods to choose from. The bigger the occasion, the bigger the dinner, like on Christmas Day.

PLAYING MUSIC

We love music and there is always some playing in the house or in the car. Iya wakes us up early in the morning every weekend, singing loudly in the shower. We always have a good singalong in the car when we are on a road trip. Our favourite types of music are afrobeats, juju, apala, and fuji.

DANCING

Where there is music playing, there is always dancing. During performances, dancers often ask the audience to join in. Bàbá Bàbá loves to dance; he stops to dance wherever he is, even if we are at the mall or the supermarket. Dances like ukwata, atilogwu nkwa umu-agbogho, and swange are often performed at festivals along with bata, which is performed to the beat of a drum.

WEDDINGS

Weddings are a big part of our culture. There is always lots of delicious food, fabulous clothing, music, and dancing. The groom often dances his way into the ceremony with his friends and they wear bowler hats and hold walking canes. Best of all, during the reception, the wedding guests throw money up in the air which falls like rain onto the newlyweds.

ENTERTAINMENT

Historically, the Yoruba people travelled from village to village putting on plays. One day they started filming them, which is how 'Nollywood' was born. It is now the second-biggest movie industry in the world, in terms of the number of films made. Nollywood movies tend to be comedies or dramas.

LET'S GET LUCKY

What do you do when your tooth falls out? What are the things that bring good luck? Here are some of ours...

HICCUPS
To get rid of hiccups, you should take a piece of thread from your clothes and put it on your head.

TOOTH
When your tooth falls out you must throw it on a rooftop. A lizard will take it and give you another one.

SNEEZING
A sneeze means someone is calling your name somewhere.

DREAMS
Anyone who sleeps on their back will have a bad dream.

Luck
Oríire
Ihu ọma
Sa'a

GOOD LUCK

If you eat beans regularly, you'll be as tall as you desire.

If you wear your clothes inside out, it can bring you good luck.

If you sweep your house in the morning, you will sweep away your bad luck and you will sleep well that night.

BAD LUCK

Blowing a whistle or whistling at night will attract snakes.

If you sweep your house at night, you will be sweeping away all of your riches.

A bat is a symbol of bad luck, especially if you see it flying in the daytime.

LET'S DREAM

Sometimes we close our eyes and dream about what we would like to be when we grow up.

Do you know what you would like to be?

Dream
Láti lá àlá
Iro nro
Yin mafarki

I WANT TO BE A NOLLYWOOD ACTRESS. MY FAVOURITE IS...

GENEVIVE NNAJI

Genevive is an actress, producer, director, and model and she has been recognised by the Nigerian government for her contributions to Nollywood. Genevive also campaigns for women's rights. I think she is beautiful and I want to be like her when I grow up. Iya and Bàbá have promised that I can start drama classes when I come home for the summer.

We all dream of travelling the world one day, and love to watch Ade hosting sports programmes as well as travel documentaries.

ADEDOYIN ADEPITAN MBE

The name Adedoyin means 'crown of honey'.

Ade is a TV presenter and sporting champion. He was born in Nigeria but moved to England as a young boy. When he was a baby, Ade contracted Polio which caused paralysis in his left leg and meant he had to use a wheelchair. This, however, did not stop him from pursuing his dream of becoming a basketball star. Ade has won medals at two Paralympics games.

I am at the top of my class in English and I like writing. Iya tells me that she would love me to be an author like...

CHIMAMANDA NGOZI ADICHIE

The name Chimamanda means '*my God will never fail*'.

Chimamanda is a well-known author whose books have won several awards internationally. Chimamanda is also known for speaking about big topics including the importance of culture in stories and female empowerment. Iya has a copy of all Chimamanda's books on her bookshelf.

Ade and Nkechi love football, their favourite player is...

BUKAYO SAKA

The name Saka means '*adds to happiness*'.

Saka is a well-known footballer, who was born and raised in England. He started playing football as a young boy and was signed to Arsenal football team at 17. Nkechi wants to be a midfielder someday, just like him.

HALIMA WANTS TO BE A SUCCESSFUL ENTREPRENEUR LIKE ALIKO DANGOTE.

Halima once tried to start a sweet shop at school with sweets she brought from home. It was going well until a teacher found out and shut her shop.

ALIKO DANGOTE

Dangote is the most successful businessman in Nigeria as well as the wealthiest man in Africa. He started in the import business before moving into manufacturing and telecommunications. Dangote is known for supporting health, education and economic empowerment in Africa.

GOODBYE

Ó DÁBÒ
(YORUBA)

SAI WANI LOKACI
(HAUSA)

KA O DI
(IGBO)

National anthem
Arise, O Compatriots
Ukwe eji eto mba   Orin Àdákọ Orílẹ́-Èdè   Wakar kasa

MEANING OF THE FLAG
Green   Two stripes represent Nigeria's natural wealth
White   Represents peace and unity

DID YOU KNOW?
Old, worn out, and dirty flags should never be displayed in public as this is considered a sign of dishonour to the country.

HISTORY

8000 BC	The oldest currently-known artefacts and stone shelters were created
700 AD–1500	Rise of Igbo, Yoruba, Edo, and Muslim civilizations
1862	Lagos Island annexed as a colony of Britain
1914	Formation of Nigeria under Governor Frederick Lugard
1929	Aba Women's riot
1959	New Nigerian currency introduced
1960	Nigeria's Independence Day
1963	Nnamdi Azikiwe became Nigeria's first president
1966	Riots in the North of Nigeria against the Igbo minority
1967–1970	The Biafran War
1971	Nigeria changed from driving on the right-hand side of the road to the left
1996	Nnamdi Azikiwe, Nigeria's first president, died
2010	Nigeria became 50 years old
2010	Twin bomb blasts at Eagle Square, Abuja
2014	Boko Haram kidnappings

THE AUTHORS

ANNA MAKANDA

Anna was born in Gweru, Zimbabwe, and raised in London, along with her older sister. Her father is Zimbabwean and her mother, Scottish. Growing up, Anna always dreamed of owning her own business. She started her career as an accountant but soon realised it was time to pursue her dreams. That was when she set up her own fitness brand.
In her spare time, you will find her spending time with family and friends, chasing after her two very energetic children, or writing a book or two!

SHARMANE BARRETT

Sharmane was born and raised in London, along with her five sisters. Her father is Jamaican and her mother, Trinidadian-English. Growing up, Sharmane was encouraged to pursue a career as a lawyer but after completing her legal studies, she soon realised that law was not for her. She began working in legal recruitment, which gave her an opportunity to live in Singapore for almost four years. Sharmane's passions are travelling and boxing – although these days there is a lot less travelling to exotic destinations, and a lot more time in the gym.

THE ILLUSTRATOR

NATÀLIA JUAN ABELLÓ

Natàlia was born in Barcelona, where she grew up with her older brother, father, and mother. She has loved drawing since she was little and was often found creating and daydreaming as a young girl. Pursuing her dream of working in a creative job, she studied to become a fashion designer but very quickly realised her real passion was to illustrate, especially children's books. Natàlia moved to the UK many years ago and now lives in a small countryside village. She loves nature, and she's happiest when taking long hikes with her partner and little doggy.

OUR GRATITUDE

We would like to say thank you and extend our gratitude to:

Everyone who helped us with the research; Gloria & Isaac Sodipo, KC Okafor, Mr Ohuonu and dear friend, Mwela Ohuonu for your advice, opinions, and most importantly, time. Thank you.

Our editor, Amber, who helped us make our facts engaging to our young readers; our copywriter, Lisa; our proof-reader, Josie; and Martyn, our wonderful designer, who not only made our books look as beautiful as they do but also helped us articulate our vision so perfectly. To our incredibly talented illustrator, Natàlia, for bringing Abiola, Adedayo, Nkechi and Halima to life, and for showcasing the magic of Nigeria.

And not forgetting all our little people for helping us pick the designs and road-testing the content.

Each other. This is a passion project for us both and to be able to share this journey with a best friend is the dream.

Anna and Sharmane

OUR MISSION

Our mission is to help ignite a child's interest in their roots and empower them to become culturally confident. We aim to do this by providing parents and caregivers factual yet engaging resources to help them teach their children about their culture and heritage.

OUR SOCIAL IMPACT

Children everywhere should have access to education. This is why for every book sold we will be donating a percentage of the proceeds to the OWMR fund which aims to support charities that do exactly that.

COPYRIGHT

First published 2021
Text Copyright ©: Anna Makanda and Sharmane Barrett
Illustration Copyright ©: Natàlia Juan Abelló

Printed in the UK
ISBN: 978-1-7399365-2-5
www.ourworldmyroots.com

All rights reserved. No part of this book may be reproduced in any form by an electronic or mechanical means, including information storage and retrieval systems, without permission in writing from the publisher, except by a reviewer who may quote brief passages in a review.

This is a work of creative nonfiction. Some parts have been fictionalised in varying degrees, for various purposes.

The publishers will be pleased to make good any omissions or rectify any mistakes brought to their attention at the earliest opportunity.

A SPECIAL THANKS TO ZACHERY MAKANDA-TANSEY, AGED 10, FOR DRAWING THIS NIGERIAN-INSPIRED PATTERN.

www.ingramcontent.com/pod-product-compliance
Ingram Content Group UK Ltd.
Pitfield, Milton Keynes, MK11 3LW, UK
UKHW050053111225
465949UK00001B/1